CW00540463

IT'S YOUR TURN
TO SPEAK

IT'S YOUR TURN TO SPEAK

A Guide to Good Speech Making

John Wade

B.T. BATSFORD LTD
LONDON

This book is dedicated to 'Absent Friends'
(coupled with the name of the Wine Waiter)

Text © John Wade 1985
Illustrations © B.T. Batsford Ltd 1985
First published 1985

All rights reserved. No part of this publication
may be reproduced, in any form or by any means,
without permission from the Publisher.

ISBN 0 7134 4697 8

Filmset by
Progress Filmsetting Limited
Printed and bound by
Butler & Tanner Ltd
Frome Somerset
for the publishers
B.T. Batsford Ltd
4 Fitzhardinge Street
London W1H 0AH

CONTENTS

ACKNOWLEDGEMENTS

I would like to thank Dabber and Paddy Davis of Associated Speakers, John Braun and Dennis Castle for their help. The drawings are by Linda Sandey.

INTRODUCTION

Very few people, apart possibly from politicians, seem to enjoy speeches. Neither those who speak, nor those who listen, are enchanted with the prospect. Strong men turn to jelly when asked to stand up in public. A chap having to deliver a talk to his colleagues will skip breakfast that morning. A lady having to thank a guest speaker at a luncheon will simply push her food about her plate, and probably not enjoy the guest speaker's talk at all. A company director having to review the past year to his shareholders at a dinner will pass up all five gourmet courses and settle for a couple of double gins instead, even if it's been a good year.

The fear of speeches works both ways, though. Why should the thought of having to sit through a speech fill us with terror? Why do those who organize functions at which there are to be speeches implore those chosen to speak, to 'keep it short'? After all, we should look forward to being instructed, or amused, or preferably both. 'Long-winded', 'pompous', and, worst of all, 'boring', are the words which unfortunately come to mind when public speaking is mentioned.

We live in an age in which communication has never been so easy or so swift. Thanks to television and radio, everyone is expected to have an instant opinion about everything and to be able to express it. A scientist, shot to the Moon, has to forget all the technical wonders that absorbed him on his way there, and on his arrival tell the world about it live on television, in words easily understood. We are all potential public speakers now,

9

and had better come to terms with it. Whether we have to speak before our business colleagues, at a church social, to a residents' association, at a Tupperware party, or face to face with a street interviewer live on television, we have to put over our thoughts in speech.

Happily, there are rules, just as in driving a car, or cooking a meal. Adequate preparation, and anticipation of possible pitfalls, can make all the difference between a chore and a pleasurable experience, for both listener and speaker.

I'm going to give an example of the worst sort of speaker, in order that we may learn from his mistakes. I'll set him at a formal dinner, but of course for 'him' you can read 'her', and for 'dinner' you can read any occasion where one has to speak, and others have to listen.

Let's imagine, then, that we have sat through a

convivial meal at a comfortable banqueting room. The coffee cups are being cleared, and the air is full of coughing as people who only smoke a cigar twice a year light up in readiness for the speeches to come. The organizer puts the microphone in position, and announces: 'Joe Bloggs, who will propose the toast to the Company'.

Joe Bloggs stands up and straightaway has to adjust the microphone for height, an action not made easier by the fact that he already has his freshly-lit cigar in his right hand, and his speech notes in the other. He starts to utter words, but they are inaudible beyond his immediate neighbours. He then bangs the mike and blows into it, while glaring around looking for the hapless man who is in charge of the sound system. This efficient sound engineer, who is in fact the Italian head waiter, turns the volume up so that the first audible words heard by the audience, and probably by the people in the pub two streets away, are 'This bloody thing isn't working'.

These hazards over, Joe Bloggs starts in earnest:

> Your Worshipful Mayor and your Good Lady; Mr Chairman; Colleagues; Ladies and Gentlemen. Standing here I'm reminded of the time when Mr Charles of Accounts visited a lady of ill-repute...

and he goes on with a tedious blue joke which in any case had been heard on a television repeat two weeks previously. Joe now launches into his prepared speech, but as he can't read his notes without his glasses, he has to stop everything while he searches for them.

We won't dwell on the actual content of the speech, most of it being statistics and faint patronizing praise for his colleagues seated at the top table. Joe has been told, though, that he must end his speech with a big laugh, so he now sets about recounting a story, cleverly inserting the names of people present, at which he had laughed on the way to the dinner when he heard it on his car radio. As it doesn't get a laugh (most of the guests had had their car radios on too), he decides to try

11

another, saucier joke. This gets a small reaction, so he tries a saucier joke which gets a better reaction, upon which he has the good sense to sit down. After a hurried whisper from his organizer, he abruptly rises again and actually proposes the health of the Company. Seated again, he forgets that the mike is still in front of him, and remarks to his neighbour that the audience was a bit stupid tonight.

Of course, that was an exaggeration. Or was it? I wrote it that way, but a friend reading the manuscript of this remarked that it was just like an estate agents' dinner he had attended quite recently. Joe Bloggs could have given a good speech had he taken some trouble beforehand. Just about every mistake he made could have been avoided by forethought.

Let's go through it again, and try to learn how Joe could have enjoyed the warm praise of his guests, instead of heading as soon as he could for the bar where he had to buy his own scotch before pleading a headache and returning home in time for the ten o'clock news.

To begin with, Joe should have *checked the microphone* himself for voice level before the guests came in, and at the same time made sure that it was at the height he wanted it. I'll have a lot more to say about mikes later, but those two elementary checks would have saved him much trouble later. It is, after all, within the first seconds of standing up that the speaker needs all the command he can get. In those first moments people's minds are being made up as to whether or not they like the speaker's suit, his tie, his voice, and even his face. To ruin those first impressions over lack of a few moments' preparation is to invite self-destruction.

Assuming that all had been well with the sound system, Joe should not have stood up to speak with his cigar going. Unless you are a George Burns, who has been timing his lines between puffs of a cigar all his long working life, *don't try it*. At best the ash will fall into your brandy, and other possible hazards include choking and setting the table on fire.

12

INTRODUCTION

Speech notes will have a section to themselves, but a very basic commonsense rule is that if you normally wear glasses to read, *then wear them*. If you don't normally need them, but are doubtful about your ability to read at arm's length under stress, then print your notes on pieces of card in large felt-pen characters.

The first words you speak should be to the *dignitaries present*, and there are very strong rules about exact forms of address.

Again, I'll be going into it in depth later (page 49), but getting a person's title or name wrong can cause more hostility than almost anything. It was Dale Carnegie in his *How to Win Friends and Influence People*, who stated that there were no sweeter words for people to hear than their own names. Getting any part of that wrong has the reverse effect, and you could be the wittiest speaker alive yet still antagonize your listeners by getting the name or title wrong. Again, homework would have saved the situation.

To begin your speech with a laugh is a good idea, but only, please, *if you are a naturally funny person*. To have an audience laughing is one of the most pleasant experiences you can enjoy, but it is not given to all of us to be funny, which is why we pay those who make us laugh consistently a great deal of money. A good, amusing story, well told, is a joy always, but avoid retelling anything that has been on radio or television in the past month or two.

Anecdotes about people present are fine, providing they *don't embarrass in any way*. Any sort of questionable material must be avoided, and by no means everyone at a function likes jokes about sex, even although such jokes do get a laugh from some people. As a speaker you have no knowledge of the prejudices and personal feelings of individuals in your audience, and cannot afford to alienate anyone. Therefore the rule on material is simple — *if in doubt, cut it out.*

INTRODUCTION

As I understand it, a speaker's job is to *inform and amuse*. It is a comedian's job to get laughs. One of the best speakers I've heard is a director of a large and respected chain of stores. He tells about the growth of the firm, its policies, how it deals with those it serves, and those who serve in it. His speech takes about twenty minutes and has probably three light chuckles in it. It could be the dullest thing in the world, but because only he can tell the story properly, and he does it with clarity and authority, it becomes riveting stuff.

✻ ✻ ✻ ✻

You don't have to be funny to be a successful speaker. On the other hand, there is no doubt that humour helps, but only if it comes naturally to you. You have been asked to speak because you have something to say which no-one else present can say. Therefore *deliver your message clearly, and sit down when you've done it*. Don't sit down, however, until you have done what you set out to do, namely in this case, propose the toast to the Company. This done, and with the assembly on its feet, glass in hand, you can sit down, confident that you've done your job, relieved that you can now set about enjoying your cigar, your drink, and the rest of the evening.

Chapter One

PREPARING TO SPEAK

It's happened at last! After all those years of sitting patiently through the speeches of others, knowing how much more witty and incisive you would be in the circumstances, suddenly you have received an invitation to make a speech yourself. Your talents have been acknowledged, albeit belatedly. You smile to yourself the self-deprecating smile you will be wearing as you sit down amidst the thunderous applause after the event. Beware. That feeling will fade a little each day as the function comes nearer. Doubts will flicker at the back of your mind and become more insistent daily. Will they understand your subtle humour? Should you try to be funny at all? Were you the first choice as speaker anyway?

As the day draws nearer you take refuge in the thought that you can always go sick, although the fact that your wife has already bought her new dress for the occasion and booked her hair appointment rather puts a damper on even that idea. Even at this late stage the best thing to do is to recognize that, just like any job of work, it can all be made easier by adequate preparation. There's still time for some homework.

When you receive an invitation to speak at a function, ask for all the arrangements to be *confirmed to you in writing*. Armed with a letter from the organizer, you are less likely to turn up at the wrong place on the wrong day, wearing the wrong sort of attire. The day before the event I always try to telephone the organizer to reassure him that I have not contracted measles, and this 'phone call also reassures me that the whole event hasn't been cancelled without my knowing. Don't think that can't happen either!

Research

With your invitation to speak will surely have come your instructions as to what you are to speak about, how long you are allowed to do it, what to wear (formal or informal), and who the other principal guests will be. Try to find out in addition how your audience is to be made up:

   Will it be a mixed audience?

   Will they be mainly young or old?

   Will they be heavily religious in any particular
   persuasion?

   How many will there be?

This information will help you to pitch the level of your speech, and especially help you to avoid making the wrong jokes in the wrong place. Remarks about 'The Little Woman' to a crowd of feminists will make you as popular as a ham sandwich at a Jewish wedding, just as reminiscences of the Blitz in 1941 will raise no eyebrows amongst an audience made up of youngsters who don't know who Frank Sinatra was.

As to the actual content of your speech, it doesn't matter whether you are to Propose the health of the happy couple, Oppose a projected motorway construction, or reply for the Visitors at a dinner, the rules are much the same, and the first such rule is *research*.

You will have to convince your audience that you have been chosen to make this speech because you are the best qualified person to do so. Therefore you will need as many facts as you can get on your subject. You can be selective later on when you make your final decision as to the content of your speech, but to start with simply *assemble as much information* as you can on all aspects of your subject.

If you are to talk about a person, *interview* relations,

spouse, colleagues and friends, making notes as you do so. If you are to talk about a society or organization, *get all the literature* you can about it. Go to the secretary of that society, to your local library, to the local newspaper, and collect facts. Don't ever rely on hearsay, as that can lead to terrible trouble on the night if someone better informed than you feels moved to interrupt and correct your last statement. All your credence will have gone, and the best oratory in the world won't be able to rescue you. Dates, times, places and names are what you want at this stage.

While you are at it, keep an eye or ear open for any *anecdotal material* relating to the subject, and also for *suitable quotations*. Libraries are full of volumes of collected quotations, all indexed under subjects. Use books of after-dinner stories, also indexed, with care, remembering that other people read them too, and the stories must have been around a while ever to have got between hard covers. Such books are very handy, though, as memory-joggers.

Constructing the Speech

You now have the title of your speech, or its principal message, written at the top of a sheet of paper, and a mass of notes. Next you have to filter this through, discarding what you consider to be the least relevant or interesting bits, before you can start to assemble the actual speech. It is stating the obvious to say that a speech has a beginning, an end and a middle. I always feel that there are two middle sections, one in which you, as it were, sow the seeds, and the other where you start to reap the nurtured growth. With a properly constructed opening, and a closing that leaves no-one in any doubt that you've finished, you have your speech.

How Many Words?

How many words should go into a speech? Obviously we all speak at different speeds, but a rule-of-thumb guide is to reckon that a sheet of A4 will hold about four hundred words if typed with double spacing. These will take about two and a half minutes to deliver aloud. Thus a thousand words will take two and half sheets of A4 double-spaced, and will take about seven and a half minutes to deliver. For a ten-minute speech, reckon about four sheets of A4 paper, double-spaced. Don't forget, though, that applause and laughter take time, and without being unduly optimistic, it might be wise to add a minute or two mentally if you are including some humorous items.

Good and Bad Grammar

If you write your speech in *short sentences* you will stand a better chance of keeping to the point. We've all probably suffered the speaker who rambles away along the lines:

> As I look around this room, and what an elegant room it is by the way, so much better than the one we used last year, and I gaze upon the well-dressed assembly—isn't it wonderful how the ladies seem to get younger as we get older?—I'm reminded of an incident that I witnessed last Wednesday, or was it Thursday? in which....

Writing short sentences will keep the attention of your listeners, and point up the content of your speech. It should also keep your grammar under control.

Without being pedantic, it is as well to follow the *rules of grammar*. Why jar some members of your audience with a split infinitive when it is just as easy to get right? 'Boldly to go' is no more difficult to say than 'To boldly go', and should offend no-one. To end a sentence with a preposition is technically wrong, but sometimes the verbal ingenuity of avoiding doing so can detract from your actual message. Remember Winston Churchill's classic 'Ending a sentence with a preposition is something up with which I will not put'.

Clichés and Metaphors

Now at this moment in time, let's have a few words

about clichés. Clichés are something *to be avoided* like the plague. They simply go in one ear and out the other. That eminent guardian of our language, Eric Partridge, said that clichés were 'substitutes for thinking'. They stick out like a sore thumb and bore the audience to tears. It is therefore as plain as a pikestaff and as clear as the nose on your face that old hackneyed phrases that everyone knows by heart are not going to rivet your audience to their seats. A little originality in your descriptions will be worth all the tea in China.

Clichés are not limited to the old familiar ones. As I write it is hardly possible to hear a politician, Trade Union leader or business executive speak on the radio without saying 'At the end of the day', or 'This is a different ball game'. In a way such phrases are even worse than the more established ones because they suggest the last time the speaker actually thought about what he was going to say.

Anything that distracts the listener from your speech is counter-productive. Clichés, 'jargon-speak' and the wrong mental image conjured up by the inadvertent use of a mixed metaphor tend to make the very people you are trying to impress wander off down their own mental paths. Mixed metaphors usually crop up during off-the-cuff speeches in which the speaker sets out with one metaphor in mind, switches mental tracks halfway through, and produces a phrase such as 'It is easier to lead a horse to water, than to get it through the eye of a needle', or 'A stitch in time gathers no moss'. Newspapers have a wonderful time teasing prominent speakers over their mixed metaphors, and just the other day I saw in the paper that 'The Mondale juggernaut has been brought to its knees'.

Quotations
If you are going to use a quotation, do be sure to get it right. No-one ever said 'All that glitters is not gold', and nowhere in Shakespeare will you find 'Lead on Macduff'.

Make sure, too, that the phrases preceding and following your chosen quotation don't negate the point you are making. At a big gathering for charity, for example, where all seems set fair for another record money-raising year, it might seem a good idea to quote John Owen saying 'Times change, and we change with them too', but remember that the next line goes 'How so? With time men only the more vicious grow'. Anyone in your audience knowing that will possibly be tempted to tell you so, thus destroying not only your erudition, but your whole point.

I think it's a brave and possibly foolhardy man who relies upon his memory to make a quotation in public without first looking it up. Good dictionaries of quotations cost very little, and the reward in confidence is well worth the outlay.

Given the hazards of misquoting or misapplying a quotation in English, consider even more carefully anything you might be tempted to quote in a foreign language. You might think it appropriate to use Napoleon's words 'L'Angleterre est une nation de boutiquiers', (England is a nation of shopkeepers), but unless you are terribly sure of yourself do get a fluent French speaker to check your pronunciation for you.

Winson Churchill got a lot of mileage from his mangling of foreign words, but we are not up to his standards of oratory. A great guffaw of laughter from the French delegation at your attempts might seem impolite—but adequate preparation would have prevented it.

A Retirement Speech
Having looked at some of the more obvious booby-traps in speech making, let's return to the construction of your speech, and take as an example that you have been asked to give a ten-minute address to follow an all-male luncheon, honouring a retiring member of the company for which you work. Because of the retiring chap's position in the local community,

the Mayor and the Chief Constable are to attend, as well as your own Managing Director who is to do the actual presentation at the end. That's your brief, and we'll try to trace the speech through.

Your central theme is the guest of honour—let's call him Bill Smith—and his forthcoming retirement. Keep that firmly in mind and remember that although you've known him for years, not everyone in the room will know much about him, or even about the company for which he has worked so long. Your research will have to bring out the highlights of Bill's working life. You will have to explain why the Mayor and Chief Constable have bothered to attend. It would be good to know about Bill's childhood and background before joining the firm, his hobbies and in which direction his interests will lie after his retirement.

You will have to talk then, for your preparation, with Bill's wife or someone who really knows about his early days. You will talk to his colleagues, keeping a lookout for any innocent foibles which might fill in the picture of the man at work. Did he make sculptures out of paper-clips? Was his handwriting so illegible that the girls in the typing pool drew lots as to who did his work? Affectionate references like these bring an instant warmth of familiarity to workmates, but they must be made with kindness and never a hint of malice. Get the Company Secretary to give you a reliable history of the firm if you don't already know it, and try to set Bill's work there into the whole perspective. Always bear in mind that it is to be Bill's day, not yours, so endeavour to paint an honest but warm picture of the man's working life.

Your working notes should now be ready to set into order. When you stand up you will, of course, start by addressing the company formally. Forms of address I'll go into later, but in this case you will start probably with 'Mr Chairman, My Lord Mayor, Chief Constable Higgins, and Guest of Honour, Bill Smith'. You will go on to say what your qualifications are for making the speech, how you shared an office for years and even went on joint family holidays perhaps. Using a quotation about retirement, but keeping it light, you can get to Bill's personal history (remembering, of course, that it is his retirement, not his obituary, you are celebrating) and the fact that he has many happy years ahead of him, free from daily commuting. Trace his childhood briefly, and his marriage if it will stand scrutiny. Weave his achievements within the company with world events: 'While Bill was putting our sales figures up for the first time in years, someone decided to start an oil price war...'.

Having painted the fullest picture possible of the man in the time available, it would be nice to say how much he will be missed, and that while he is on his world cruise, or growing his geraniums, the company will be hard pushed to find his replacement, even though he has been training someone for that very job. Having done your best for nine minutes, you will spend the last minute wishing Bill luck, and calling upon your Managing Director who will make the actual presentation. 'Gentlemen, our Managing Director', will be your cue to sit down.

Notes

You will notice that I haven't said much about the physical form your notes will take on the day. Ideally, of course, a speaker shouldn't use notes at all, but on one-off occasions such as this, you must have the facts to hand. Typewritten sheets of paper often hide your face from view, can look awfully daunting to the audience, and tend to flop about and rustle into the microphone. I advocate using *postcard-sized pieces of card* with headings, dates and names written in large letters in felt-tip pen. Armed with a small pack of such cards, which easily slip into handbag or pocket, you can rearrange items at will up until the last minute. As you speak, you simply slip the top card onto the table or under the pack as you finish with its contents.

Carry a spare blank card or two so that you can make

notes during other speeches which you might want to refer to. If there are previous speakers, they often give you a cue into something that you had already meant to say, so that you can pay them a compliment gracefully as you say 'Chief Constable Higgins mentioned Bill Smith's great ability as a J.P., which reminds me of a time when we went out...' and so on with your own story.

Although I don't like speeches that are simply read out as a paper directly from a prepared script—they tend to stay on the paper and not come to life, as the speaker can't get eye contact with his audience—I am a great believer in *saying the speech aloud* to yourself at the end of its preparation. You may feel a bit embarrassed as you speak in full voice with only yourself as an audience, but the exercise is invaluable. Not only does it give you a close idea of the timing and its length, but it also shows up difficult words. Often words which look good on paper simply don't work when you come to say them aloud. Either they sound clumsy, or you trip over them. Sometimes just rearranging a couple of words will make a whole phrase sound better, and it is the sound you are concerned with. Even skilled professionals such as BBC radio announcers keep a watchful eye open for words that might stop the smooth flow, often putting in a substitute word.

Don't have any inhibitions then. Send everybody out of your home or office for half an hour, and say your speech aloud to yourself. If you have a cassette tape recorder it might be useful to use it to play the speech back afterwards. That is when you will notice any possible stumbling blocks in words, or any jerky change of direction in the subject matter.

* * * *

Make sure that your research is properly done and that you have some legible, useful notes, preferably on cards. Now you can take time off from worrying about it, say nice things about your partner's appearance as you get into the car—and enjoy yourself.

Chapter Two

EFFECTIVE SPEAKING

Rehearsing

If you've never made a public speech before, the chances are that should you have followed my advice in the previous chapter and spoken your address aloud, you will have experienced a kind of unreality, particularly if you recorded it and listened to it played back. You find that you didn't sound a bit like you always thought you sounded. The voice, the accent and the timing weren't the way you intended. *Don't worry.* This has happened to us all and you are not the first person to think this way. Luckily, there are many steps you can take to make yourself sound more natural.

Play the recording back again to yourself, this time listening not so much to the content of the speech, but to the way you sound. Does you voice stay on the same level of pitch and volume throughout? A monotone will send people to sleep, so try to emulate the good actor who can make the most familiar words of Shakespeare come to life simply by using lights and shades in his voice. Try emphasizing your key words or phrases by *speaking more slowly.* Start each sentence on a high level, and never drop your voice at the end of a line. The very tone of your voice can convey whether you are being deadly serious, or gently amusing.

Listen again to your recording and see if you can hear your breathing. Actors and singers know that *good breathing* can be the key to everything. Gulping for air in the middle of a sustained passage of music or prose can destroy all the magic, so the professional takes great steps to overcome possible traps. This does not mean that you have to take in great gulps of air audibly, but rather that you use your punctuation marks as breathers. This is usually instinctive—we do it all the time. The last thing I want to do is to make you aware of every breath you take, but, on the other hand, if when you listen to yourself on tape you notice that you showed signs of running out of steam, try rephrasing the sentence to give you a practical breathing space. Speaking to a room full of people is quite hard physical work, and you don't want to suggest to your audience that you have a bronchial problem. So take your time, and remember that the pauses are just as important as the words.

If you read your speech at proper speaking level, it is unlikely that you will have started to 'um' and 'er'. This sort of thing happens when you are simply unsure of what you are going to say next, and are groping for words. Listen to people on radio interviews who preface their every answer with 'Well', or 'Right', before getting to what they actually want to say. Such words are totally unnecessary and again tend to make the listener switch off mentally. If you need time to think—and in your own prepared speech you shouldn't—don't feel obliged to fill the air with

28

'non-words'; just make a slightly longer pause before restarting.

You may find that in part of your recorded speech you tended to rush your words, and this might be because you yourself subconsciously considered them less important, and wanted to get through them quickly. If you really thought that, then perhaps the whole passage is better left out altogether. If something is worth saying, then it should be *said with conviction.*

Watch out for what I call *pompous speech language.* Some people who normally speak perfectly plain acceptable English, tend to drop into a special sort of language for a speech. Instead of 'getting around' a problem, they will 'circumnavigate' it. Instead of 'now', or 'at present', it becomes 'at this moment in time'. Often this only confuses the audience and makes the speaker appear to be trying to over-impress.

One more word upon hearing yourself on tape. It might seem to you that you have a pronounced *regional accent,* and you don't like the sound of it too much. A few years ago this might have been important, but please don't worry about it now. That is the way you have talked all your life, and it is a part of your make up. Certainly you shouldn't start trying to straighten it out at this stage into what you might consider an acceptable accent, or what used to be called 'Broadcasting English'. Be yourself, and if you feel like it, even cash in on it a bit. Be a homey Yorkshireman, or a lyrical Welshman. Your audience have asked *you* to speak about *your* subject, so don't start trying to be somebody else.

Now with all that in mind, try another recording, at full speech level, remembering that when you come to do it on the occasion it will almost certainly be in a totally unfamiliar atmosphere. You will be standing up in a strange room, probably at a table at which you've been eating, and you will probably have to cope with a microphone. So when you do your next rehearsal try to get something of the feel of the real occasion. Stand at a table, and if you don't have a mike to hand, put a table lamp or some other object in front of you to simulate it. Just standing like that will show you how to hold your cue cards without hitting the mike or knocking your glass of wine over—yes, set that too, because it will be there on the night.

Your hands might suddenly seem enormous. It's amazing how we live with our hands perfectly compatibly until we stand up in public. Actors have the same trouble. The answer is simple, of course, inasmuch as your hands are attached to the end of your arms, and that's where they stay. You'll probably have your notes in one hand anyway, but the other does not have to be stuck into a pocket, placed on your hip or waved about in expansive gestures (remember that glass of wine). Just keep you hand to your side until you need it to change cards. Avoid fiddling with the mike. Once it's set, leave it alone.

Some people don't have trouble only with their hands. Where should their eyes go? Sometimes they will be on the notes of course, but unless what is being read is absolutely earth-shattering, the audience's attention will soon wander if the eyes stay down. 'The eyes are the windows of the soul' it has been said, obviously by someone who had never met a convincing liar, but nonetheless it is with the eyes that you gain someone's attention, and hold it.

As your voice is being projected to the back of the room, so then too should your eyes look towards the middle distance most of the time, but moving around the room too, near and far, without actually fixing upon any one person. Just occasionally, during a pause or a laugh, you can engage someone's eyes for a moment, but otherwise keep them taking in the whole room, avoiding actual eye contact.

One reason I advise against looking directly at anyone during a speech is that to others, as well as the person being looked at, it might seem that this particular piece is being said to them alone, and it might embarrass them. Another reason is that in engaging someone's eye unexpectedly, you yourself might be thrown off balance if they should wink back, or drop their eyes to the table. If you keep your notes at chest height and your head well up, your eyes will be visible to the audience, and your voice will stand a better chance of carrying.

If there is no mike, you will find yourself having to *project your voice* to the back of the room. Projecting does not mean shouting, and if you've not had to do it before, try to get into the room before the function starts, stand at your place, and talk clearly to the back table. If your partner or a colleague can listen for you, you will know in advance just how much voice to give it. With no mike, consonants become most important. They are important anyway if you want to be heard easily, but doubly so when you are trying to reach a long way. 'T', 'D' and 'V' are the consonants most frequently dropped in common speech, so pay attention to these particularly.

On the Night

My early Boy Scout training led me to try to be prepared for almost any eventuality, so I carry with me on speaking engagements the following emergency tool kit, every item of which I assure you I've used, but more often used on someone else's behalf:

Aspirin
Safety pins
Nail file/Clippers
Sticking plaster
Toothbrush
Freshener tissues
Paper handkerchiefs

Nothing in that list is very big, but, oh how valuable when needed!

The Use and Abuse of Alcohol

Having tested the room for sound, and got acquainted with how the room will look to you as you speak, you can now join the rest of the company for the reception and the first part of the dinner. You will want to be seen at your best, and feel at your best, while you speak, so *take it easy with the drinks.* You may think that a few glasses will help to loosen the tongue and put you on top of the world, but in fact drink can well make you over-confident, and ruin your judgement and your timing. By all means enjoy yourself when your job is over, but until then I suggest that you take it gently.

As to the quality of your voice when speaking, certain drinks work against the voice. Most spirits will dry your throat up. Many singers sip a glass of port before working, but water has always been the most reliable lubricant—not the fizzy sort though, remembering the burps and hiccups that can occur.

32

A friend of mine had a near disaster at a function where he was engaged to speak, all due to excess hospitality. He had a bad cold, and on the train he dosed himelf with one of those proprietary cold cures that work on a timer inside you, so that the effect lasts over a period of hours.

It was a Ladies' Luncheon Club he was due to address, and on his arrival some of the ladies took pity on his obvious condition and fed him liberal 'medicinal' scotch before lunch, kindly also sending a few to his place at table during the actual lunch. Not many people knew then of the combined effects of cold cures and alcohol, but his audience watched with mixed emotions as our speaker not only had a problem with words, but with his legs too. After a few incoherent sentences, he gradually disappeared under the table.

It is greatly to the credit of those ladies that they promptly booked a room for him in the hotel and packed him off to bed to sleep everything off. It could have gone badly against him, but within a month or two he was able to attend their luncheon again, this time in full control, and be his usual entertaining self.

The same precepts that apply to drink apply to food. You won't want to stand up to speak with indigestion, and find your golden sentences punctuated with the odd hiccup or a suppressed belch. Particles of food left between the teeth can be a menace too, especially if you wear dentures, so carry a toothbrush if possible. Most airports and big stores now sell small toothbrushes that are pre-pasted, in sealed containers. You use them and throw them away—just fine for our purpose.

Nerves

Nerves may be playing you up a bit as the dinner progresses, but please resist the urge, as I've said, to have a couple of stiff drinks to calm you down. It's much better to take some deep breaths. Towards the end of the meal, I try to 'switch off' from the assembly

and spend just a few moments breathing deeply and concentrating on the job in hand.

Don't do this, however, during the preceding speeches, or you might miss something important, such as the fellow before you doing your best anecdote. What precedes you has a great bearing on what you will do, so use the time fully. Watch for places in the room where the laughter sounds loudest, or where some heckler seems to lurk. Very often in a preceding speech you'll hear something that bears on what you are going to say, and can turn this to advantage as we've already seen. Always listen attentively to other speakers, and be seen to be doing so. You will want their undivided attention when you speak, so it is only courtesy to listen to them without obviously making last-minute notes to your own offering.

Last-minute Alterations

You must be prepared to make some last-minute changes in your speech. Obviously if a speaker has already used a joke that you were going to do, you will have to delete it and substitute another, and as good jokes are hard to come by, this might not be as easy as it sounds. It might well turn out, though, that a remark from an earlier speaker will give you a natural lead into something you were going to say anyway, and it helps a lot if you can capitalize on it by saying 'I was glad to hear Mr Smith mention so-and-so, and it reminded me of...' and so on, into your own story.

During your speech you might find the attention of the audience wandering, and you might have to rejig things a bit to get them back. Bring an amusing story forward to get a laugh before going back into your subject. Look for signs of restlessness in your audience, and try to anticipate their mood. Coughing is a sign. Not just one isolated cough, but a number of them. Musicians know well that an outbreak of coughing during a concert signals boredom, just as they know they have held their audience if there is no disturbance at all.

Standing Up to Speak

When your turn comes to speak, stand up, plant your feet a little apart, take the briefest of pauses to survey the room, and start clearly on your introductory remarks. During this time you can take a quick check around the room and see if everyone can hear. People who can't hear often lean forward to catch the words, or even cup their ears with their hands. If you see this, then project your voice further.

Here I should like to pass on a tip from a lady I know who speaks often in public. Like many ladies, she sometimes wears new shoes for the first time at functions, and, knowing how new shoes can hurt, especially after several hours in a warm room, she takes hers off when she stands up to speak. No-one can see, of course, and it certainly must help a great deal. Dresses with floppy sleeves that might dangle in the glassware, and heavy jewellery that bangs against the mike stand are also hazards you can do without. Men can avoid the irritating habit of hitching up their trousers by wearing braces.

One further word on the length of your speech. Over the years I have found just once in a while that on sitting down at the conclusion there has been one part of the room applauding more loudly than the others. If this happens to you, don't get carried away with your own apparent success. Often at places where a guest speaker is a regular item at meetings, such as Round Table or Rotary Clubs, there is a clandestine sweepstake on the exact length of time the speaker will take. That extra cheer at the end is usually from the chap whose prediction coincided with your actual time. It's all good-natured, and I find that if I explain afterwards that I knew what a generous chap he was, and timed my speech according to what I thought he would have predicted, it often results in a double scotch being thrust gratefully into my hand.

Mostly Microphones

Most places these days have a mike and an adequate sound system, although that doesn't mean that there is always somebody there competent to make it work properly. It therefore becomes even more important that you get into the room before the guests arrive, and try the mike yourself. Set it where it will be and get the mike head into a position about ten inches from your mouth and slightly below it. This way your face should not be obstructed from view, and you should be audible throughout the room. Bear in mind that the level at which you speak in an empty room will have to be put up a shade when the room is full, but the chap operating it should know about that. A mike is an *aid to speaking,* not an essential, so please don't put the thing right on to your lips in the manner of some pop singers, as it will distort your speech badly.

In the best of worlds there would always be someone on hand to sit by the amplifier and adjust the control level to each speaker's requirements. The best hotels have just such a person, and the quality of sound reproduction is so important to singers that many carry their own sound engineer and equipment with them. We don't need that, but we do need to make sure that the thing is properly arranged before the speeches start. Should you get unlucky, and despite all your careful efforts when you stand up finally find it's either too soft or too loud, get it adjusted during your preliminary remarks, and wait until it is. There's nothing worse than trying to get into your mainsteam against a howling sound system.

You'll never please everyone on sound levels, by the way, and in the end you will know how you are being heard by the way you are being received. If you see people at a distant table getting restive and whispering to each other, the chances are that they can't hear you and have given up trying. Your normal conversational voice is not enough for anything other than the most sophisticated sound system, so you will need to slow up a bit, and project your voice to the back of the room as if there is no mike. As I said, a mike is an aid to speaking, but can only reproduce what is put into it in the first place.

Check on the mike stand as to how to raise or lower the head. Some work with a twist-screw device that you loosen by hand, raise or lower the head and then tighten again yourself. Others have a sort of hydraulic device where you have only to raise or lower the stem without having to turn anything. I once spoke at a function where I had made all the preparations necessary, and yet when I came to speak, the previous speaker had obviously been much taller than me, so I had to lower the stand a little. It was one of the hydraulic sort, but nobody had told me it had been freshly oiled, so when I depressed it a fair squirt of oil shot up my arm, covering my hands, my notes, and a good bit of tablecloth too.

Mention of a tablecloth reminds me of another hazard which reads like a section of a television comedy, but I assure you that it has happened on more than one occasion in real life. During the meal the speaker had tucked his napkin into the top of his trousers to prevent its falling on the floor. In doing so he had also caught the hem of the tablecloth, so that when he stood to speak the entire tablecloth rose at the same time. Such slapstick didn't help his first few minutes of speaking one bit.

As I've said before, once you have the mike set properly, please leave it alone and *don't fiddle with it*. Please don't tap the mike to see if it is working; not only

does this do damage inside the mike's head sometimes, but if there is a sound man with headphones on in a control box, you will give him a very nasty headache. Just speak into it, and you'll soon know if it's not on. Some, but by no means all, mikes have an 'on-off' switch, which is always worth checking.

No two functions are ever the same. The conditions are always different, from the layout of the tables or seating and the numbers present, to the equipment available. As you will only have one chance to get it right, it follows that anything you can do beforehand to ensure smooth running is time well spent. Murphy's Law, which states that anything that can go wrong, will, applies more to one-off occasions than anything else, but at least you can shorten the odds by suitable preparation.

You may be asked to speak at a business promotion or sales conference, and may be bewildered by the vast range of hardware all over the platform. These days there is often a cinema screen on one side for slides and movies, and a large video screen on the other. There will be a couple of lecterns, each with a mike, and cables disappearing into the body of the hall, linking the whole works with men who actually project the slides, movies and videos and work the sound.

You might well find a box on the floor with a thin stand rising out of it, on top of which is a tilted sheet of glass. This too will have a cable sticking out of it leading to someone actually working the gadget. This is an auto-cue, beloved now of Presidents and Prime Ministers. It enables the speaker to read his speech word for word without appearing to have any notes. In fact all the words are projected on to the tilted glass screen which seems transparent to the audience. The script is transmitted on to the screen at the speed at which the speaker talks—or that is the theory at least—and it all seems quite worry-free. By all means use it if it's offered to you, but I feel that any mechanical aid, including microphones, can come between you and your audience. The more freedom of movement you have, and the more time to look at your listeners, the better your contact will be.

* * * *

I hope you will not be frightened by the apparent amount of preparation I've suggested for a smooth evening. None of the measures takes long, and if as a result you are relaxed when you stand up to speak, so will your listeners be. Yours is just one part of an evening which, taken together with the quality of the food, the service, and the music if there is any, go to make up an entertaining night out for everybody.

At this point I can now relax myself, picturing you in my mind's eye with your rehearsed speech notes in your pocket, together with your letter telling you where and when the function is to be. You are comfortably dressed, and you have your tiny 'First-aid' kit with you. Have an enjoyable evening, and remember the cardinal rules of public speaking:

Stand Up
Speak Up
Shut Up.

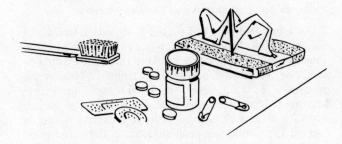

Chapter Three

AFTER-DINNER SPEECHES

Of all the forms that speaking in public can take, it is the formal after-dinner speech which seems to generate the most fears, not only with those who make them, but those who have to listen. Possibly it is that very word 'formal' that causes part of the trouble. A look at the printed menu set before every diner will usually disclose a list of speeches as follows:

The Queen, or The Loyal Toast
Toast to the Society
Response
The Ladies and Visitors
Response

Taking them in order, the *Loyal Toast* is a straightforward announcement, made usually by the Chairman, who will rise and say 'Ladies and Gentlemen—The Queen'. The guests will stand, reply 'The Queen', and sit down again, after which the Chairman may give permission for those who wish to, to smoke.

The *Toast to the Society* is often proposed by a guest speaker, but not necessarily so. This need not be a long speech, unless it is to be the event of the evening. The *Response* to it is often made by the Chairman or President of the Society, and, again, need not take long.

The *Toast to the Ladies and/or Visitors* is proposed by a member of the Society, and after naming many of the guests the speech will become an introduction to the principal speaker, often supplying background and biographical material about him or her.

AFTER DINNER SPEECHES

The *Response* will usually be the main speech of the evening, at the end of which the speaker will thank the hosts on behalf of all the guests.

Sometimes the Chairman will reply briefly to the guest speaker, but this is by no means obligatory.

Length

The length of speeches must obviously depend upon how much time is available. On the above list, if each speaker before the principal one takes ten minutes, and the principal guest takes twenty, the total is already pretty near an hour. If dancing is to follow the speeches, then time is a strong factor. Assuming everyone is seated for dinner as early as 7.30 pm, the actual meal should be over, with coffee on the table, by about 8.45. The speeches should be over, at the above reckoning, by 9.45, allowing dancing to start by 10.00.

This schedule would be too tight for a dinner without dancing, at which, as the speeches are the entertainment, there can be more leeway. Brevity, however, has always been the soul of wit, and it is far better for people to come up to you afterwards saying 'Oh, I do wish you could have gone on for longer', than to be made to feel that you have kept them from the real business of the evening, the drinking and dancing.

Even with functions at which the speeches are the main event of the evening, it is worth bearing in mind the tale of the visiting American who came to address a dinner to mark the end of a school year, and to honour those leaving. He took as his theme his own Alma Mater, the illustrious college of Yale, and used each letter of the word to emphasize his points. Thus he started with 'Y' for Youth, on which he expounded for about twenty minutes, getting then to 'A' for Ambition, and in due course to 'L' for Learning and finally to 'E' for Establishment. As he at last sat down the Chairman was heard to remark that it was just as well the speaker hadn't attended the Massachusetts Institution of Technology.

43

Content

As to the content of a speech, it is in that Response to the Ladies or Visitors, that a problem might arise. All the other speeches have specific directions in which to go and we've seen in an earlier chapter how good research can smooth the path. The Response to the Visitors is a wide open field in which you can wander at will. Of course, if you are invited because of your celebrity value, as Author, TV Personality, Scientist, Traveller or Politician, you can just string along your own favourite anecdotes, which are what people want to hear. You have to decide whether to be serious or funny. You might want to grab the chance to get a personal message across, or you might set out to be controversial and risk a bit of atmosphere afterwards. Whatever you do, the end of the speech is fixed. Like any good guest, you must thank your host graciously, and in doing so make clear that you are including all the other guests. What comes before is, as I've said, entirely up to you, but generally it is advisable to keep your speech light and courteous. A little mental stimulation can be welcome, although before straining any IQs it should be remembered that your listeners will have been enjoying a drink or two, and will probably be in need of some relaxation.

It is never bad to *stay within your brief* and actually make a reply on behalf of the visitors. Name a few of them perhaps, and tie in a story which could relate to them. If there is a really good story about a guest there, then use it, but only with the following provisions. Firstly, it should be genuinely funny to everyone, and not just to the participants. Secondly, make sure that it cannot possibly offend either the subject of the story or his escort, and that he won't mind your telling the story. Thirdly it is best if the person about whom the story is being told comes out well, and you are the butt of any loss of dignity.

Humour

Make capital out of being a guest, and possibly a stranger in the town. Your attempts to find the venue and get the car parked can be amusing, paticularly if the hotel is in the middle of a notorious one-way system. Make the humour your own ineptitude though. People are very sensitive about their own towns, and remarks about them from outsiders. 'A funny thing happened on the way to the theatre' was a good ploy by comedians.

Humour is a tricky business. I mentioned some of the possible pitfalls in the Introduction. I have strong feelings about sexual jokes, even in all-male company, bad language jokes, racial jokes and funeral jokes. It is no good offending anyone at a social function, and one can be misled by comments afterwards. The chap who comes up to you and tells you how funny your joke about the Irish prostitute was, may well be the first to get back to his table and friends and criticize you for the choice of tale. It's simply not worth it. I've attended all-male dinners at which the chairman beforehand has hinted heavily that I could get quite strong if I wanted, only to find afterwards that for every chap who suggests that a few blue gags might have been appreciated, there is another who thanks me for not insulting his intelligence.

How do you know if a joke or story is fit to tell in public? My personal yardstick is whether I would tell it in mixed company of all ages around my own dinner table. Of course there is a time and a place for good strong jokes: with trusted friends or around a bar for instance. But the chaps, and ladies too, who laugh loudly around a bar might not be at all pleased were you to do the same story in public. 'If in doubt—cut it out', a phrase I used in the Introduction, is an old one from the days of variety theatres when a comic might try and slip a saucy one in to a crowded house. He'd get a huge laugh at the time, but wonder why he wasn't booked back.

I hear people use words and stories on television, broadcast to millions of people's homes, that I wouldn't use in my own club, let alone in public. However, a television set does have an 'off' button, whereas if you are speaking in public your listeners have no choice other than to listen. If you've ever seen a speaker get frozen out by a hostile audience, it is not a pleasant thing, and certainly not calculated to help a social evening along its pleasant way, which should be the intention.

Another touchy subject to be avoided is that of death. It's odd how many funny stories are concerned with death and funerals, but I don't think they have any place in after-dinner speeches, except possibly at the Undertakers' and Pallbearers' Annual Ball. In case you think I'm over-sensitive I'll give you a personal example. Two months after my father's death I took my mother along to a dinner as a gentle evening out. It was her first time at any sort of public function since my father's death, and as luck would have it, the first speaker told two stories about coffins straight off. Not only was my mother a bit upset, but those around her were upset for her. The speaker probably doesn't know to this day why he lost the respect of a number of his audience that night.

I seem to have said a great deal on what not to speak about. What is there left? Just about everything. If you are stuck for an idea to set you off, see if the day you are doing your speech is an anniversary of some important person or event. There are some invaluable books of dates available in your library, and in paperback, and I've often found inspiration in them. For instance, by referring to my *Encyclopaedia of Dates* I can tell my listeners that 'in the year 1877 when this eminent society was formed, Queen Victoria was proclaimed Empress of India, Anna Sewell wrote Black Beauty, Brahms wrote his second symphony in D Major, and Edison patented the phonograph'. It gives people a little thought-food, as well as putting the Society into historical perspective.

I've already mentioned books of quotations and collections of after-dinner anecdotes. Used sparingly, and as more of a trigger to fresh ideas than simply a recitation of the thoughts of other people, they can be valuable. Some of my particular favourites can be found on page 79-83.

Question and Answer Sessions

I've not discussed the idea of having a 'Question and Answer' session after your speech. Not every subject can take such treatment, but it can be fun, providing of course, that you are ready for anything. If you agree to such a session after your main speech, may I suggest that you take a couple of guests aside and ask them to have a question ready should there be a terrible silence when the Chairman announces that 'Our Guest speaker has kindly consented to answer some questions'. There might be a flood of questions of course, but it's as well to make sure of the first one, which will encourage others.

When a question comes from the room, always repeat it, as the questioner won't have a mike and not everyone will have heard it. Then answer it swiftly. Questioners often simply want to be heard, to display their own wit or knowledge. Deal with them courteously and fully. When you think you've answered enough questions, I suggest you have one story of your own in reserve that you can finish on strongly, so as to avoid the suggestion that the speech has in any way petered out.

* * * *

We started this chapter by worrying about the 'formal' dinner speeches, and I hope that we've finished it by seeing how such an event can be made amusing, informative, and totally relevant to the date on which it takes place.

Chapter Four
TITLES AND
FORMS OF ADDRESS

The first person you address when you rise to speak at a formal function will be the *Chairman*, and you will call him 'Mr Chairman' unless he happens to be a person of rank, in which case he will become 'My Lord Chairman'. If the chair is being taken by the President of whatever association it is, then you address him as 'Mr President'.

The next person you will address will be any member of the *Royal Family* who might be present, and then anyone else to whom you wish to extend a formal acknowledgement, a Mayor for instance. Your opening so far then has become 'My Lord Chairman, Your Highness, My Lord Mayor...'.

You must now include the *person to whose speech you are replying*, and finish with 'Lords [if there be any present], Ladies and Gentlemen'. Thus we have now built up for our formal dinner speech the following complete opening; 'My Lord Chairman, Your Royal Highness, My Lord Mayor, Mr Terry Wogan, My Lords, Ladies and Gentlemen'.

Don't worry, it won't happen often, and should such formidable dignitaries be there, you will be well briefed beforehand. However, let's· assume you are going to start at the top. Here's a list of the proper forms of address for persons of rank:

A ruling sovereign	Your Majesty
Member of the Royal Family	Your Royal Highness

| Duke | My Lord Duke |
| Marquis | My Lord Marquis |

All other titles are covered within 'My Lord, and 'My Lady, except:

President	Mr President
Vice President	Mr Vice President
Prime Minister	Mr (or Madam) Prime Minister, or simply Prime Minister
Archbishop	Your Grace
Bishop	My Lord Bishop
Doctor of Divinity	Reverend Sir
Dean	Very Reverend Sir
Archdeacon	Venerable Sir
Ambassador	Your Excellency
Governor	Your Excellency
Lord Mayor	My Lord Mayor
Mayor	Mr (or Madam) Mayor

Once you have referred to a person by his or her full title in your opening, you need only use 'Sir', or 'Madam' afterwards during your speech. A Knight is not a Lord, and comes under 'Ladies and Gentlemen', unless you are referring to him by name when he becomes 'Sir Robin Day'.

✳ ✳ ✳ ✳

There is a general air of relaxation these days over the strictly formal forms of address, and the organizer of the function will steer you in the right direction. However, you can never be wrong by being correct, and thanks to these pages, you are now fully equipped to deal with the situation when the gold-monogrammed invitation finally appears on your mantlepiece.

Chapter Five

SOCIAL SPEECHES
FOR SPECIAL OCCASIONS

Weddings, christenings and anniversaries are very special events to those attending, as well as those principally involved. Thus it is particularly important to see that the speeches offend nobody, and emphasize the uniqueness and solemnity of the celebration. These days many such events are recorded on sound cassette tapes, or even on video tapes, so one careless or insensitive remark is there permanently afterwards, possibly spoiling the whole souvenir.

Wedding Receptions

In Chapter One I traced through the speech to be made at the retirement of an old employee of a firm. The same rules of research apply to toasts at wedding receptions. The speeches need not be stiff and starchy, but any humour must be gentle and relevant.

It is usual to let the reception run for about an hour before the Best Man guides the Bride and Groom to a

spot near the wedding cake and calls for silence. If there is a Toastmaster or Master of Ceremonies, then that will be his function of course.

The toast to the Bride and Groom is usually proposed by the Bride's father, or a close family friend of the bride. The Groom will then reply, thanking the Bride's parents for the reception if appropriate, and also the guests for their wedding presents. He will finish by proposing a toast to the Bridesmaids.

The Best Man will respond to that toast and, in the absence of a Toastmaster, will then read the messages of good luck sent by those unable to attend. This is sometimes where a hazard can crop up. Many such messages are witty and amusing, but it is not unknown for other messages to find their way in, usually heavy with innuendo about first nights and hotel bedrooms. It's a cheap way of getting laughs and often embarrasses more than amuses. Once again—'When in doubt, cut it out'. It can happen that a real message arrives which is vulgar in content, and I'm sure that it is part of the responsibility of whoever is reading such messages to 'lose' it during the readings. If questioned later, he can always claim that it arrived too late to be included.

We all have parts of our lives that would not want made public, and the Bride and Groom are probably nervous enough, both at the occasion itself, and at the forthcoming change in their lives, without guffaws of ribald laughter coming up from sections of the room. Keep the speeches short, light and sincere, cognisant of the big step being taken. After all, the Groom probably had a stag party the night before (and maybe the Bride a hen party), during which doubtless the drink, the ribaldry and the laughter flowed freely.

Immediately after the speeches, the Bride and Groom will make the ceremonial cut in the wedding cake, and soon afterwards will leave to change into their going-away clothes. The Best Man will join the Groom when he's changed, and make sure the car is available and the luggage stowed away. As soon as the Bride is changed and ready, the Best Man will announce to the assembly that the couple are about to leave, and make sure that all the guests gather to see them off. When the Bride throws her bouquet into the crowd, and the car has departed, sometimes to the rattle of tin cans tied to it, the reception is over.

Christenings, Anniversaries and Bar Mitzvahs

The reception after a *christening* ceremony is usually a private family affair, and speeches are not required. However it might fall to one of the grandparents, or godparents, to wish the baby well, and to thank whoever laid on the food and drinks.

If a happily married couple wished to celebrate their *wedding anniversary* by holding a small dinner party, a short tribute to the couple, again thanking them for the hospitality, can be paid by a son or daughter if suitable, by an old family friend, or by whoever was Best Man at their wedding.

Those wonderful Jewish celebrations that follow the *Bar Mitzvah* or *Bat Mitzvah* ceremony for boys or girls who have reached their thirteenth birthday, have only one principal speaker, the boy or girl themselves. Although during the course of such a speech they will probably thank their parents for the party themselves, sometimes it will fall to one of the guests to do so as well as a matter of courtesy.

✻ ✻ ✻ ✻

Any festive family occasion, although obviously a time for celebration and merriment, deserves also that old-fashioned term 'dignity'. Those at the centre will appreciate such treatment at what will probably be the only time in their lives when they will receive such attention.

Chapter Six

POLITICAL SPEECHES

A great number of the words uttered in public are, for better or worse, devoted to politics. Political gatherings usually fall into one of two categories: political meetings or political debates, so let us look at the difference between the two.

Meetings

Political meetings are, as a rule, organized by one political party in order to present a candidate or a new policy document to an audience mainly of its own supporters. If it is a candidate who is to be presented on local, county or national level, he will usually be introduced by the local party Chairman, and supported by a prominent member of the party who is often the 'draw' to encourage people to attend the meeting.

The *Chairman* is the pivot at such meetings, having to implement whatever rules have been laid down for the meeting in advance, such as the length of time allocated to each speaker, the order in which they are to appear, and whether there are to be questions afterwards from the floor. Providing everyone attending the meeting knows the rules, which will be restated by the Chairman at the beginning of the meeting, there should be no problems.

Heckling from the floor is to be expected, and can be stimulating. Heckling puts the speakers on their mettle, and can serve to show those attending the candidate's ability to think on his feet. Political speakers are quite used to such interruptions, expect them, and even welcome them.

A bigger problem is the *organized claque* which can attend with the intention of causing the total break-up of the meeting, by making it impossible for any speaker to be heard at all. How the Chairman deals with such a situation is a good test of his own ability, but he is well protected, by the law if necessary. If the Chairman stands up to restore order and cannot himself get a hearing, he can suspend the meeting until the faction leaves, either by expulsion or invitation. As I've said before, the best meetings are those run by popular consensus, but when people attend the meeting with the sole purpose of disruption, heavier measures have to be taken.

Debates

Political debates are different in that under a neutral chairman the speakers from opposite sides put their points of view, and are often questioned upon those views; then those attending are invited to choose between the arguments they have heard advanced. Again, the rules under which such a debate is organized must be known to everyone beforehand, and be seen to be carried out by the Chairman.

Usually the speakers will debate a *motion* which has been agreed upon by those participating, including the Chairman. The *Proposer* will speak for an agreed length of time to his motion, followed by the *Seconder*. The *Opposer* will then speak for the same period, and his Seconder afterwards. The meeting may then be asked for questions or comments, all within a prearranged time schedule, before the principal speakers wind up their cases at the end. Now although that sounds a simple and fair formula for a civilized and intelligent debate, all too often spanners are thrown into the works by the same by-no-means always well intentioned people I mentioned earlier.

Some of those attending, skilled in the ways of debate, and fond of their own voices, will try to gain extra speaking time for their cause by raising *points of order*. Points of order should mean just that—questions regarding the conduct of the debate—not an excuse for restating a point of view under another guise. A good strong Chairman will recognize this ruse and deal with it swiftly, usually to approval from the body of the hall.

At the end of any sort of meeting or debate it is customary for someone to make a *vote of thanks* to those participating, including the Chairman. This vote of thanks will often switch the attention from the abstracts of the debate to the personalities of those involved, and can indeed send people out of the meeting in a better frame of mind.

* * * *

In theory a political debate should be the most civilized way of educating and informing people of current thinking, with the chance to participate if necessary. In practice it seems that free speech is only to be allowed by those of one's own persuasion. Radio broadcasts from the House of Commons do little to encourage standards of debating by example, but on a good day a debate in the House of Lords can still be an uplifting example of how things should be.

Chapter Seven

THE DUTIES OF
A CHAIRMAN

Anyone who has a great interest in life apart from their job, be it stamp-collecting or surfboarding, tenants' association or sports club, will probably have joined an organization of like-minded people, and will have attended local committee meetings. After a few years of diligent committee work, possibly at area or national level, it is quite likely that he or she will have been asked to become Chairman of the committee, often for a limited period of say a year or two, in recognition of the hard work put in. Thus, if a person is asked to become Chairman of an organization, it is likely that he will have had some experience of the conduct of meetings, both formal and informal. This does not, unfortunately, mean that he will make a good job of being Chairman, because the Chairman's job entails the exercising of a certain amount of power, and power does funny things to people.

Quite simply, the Chairman is in charge of the function, be it a dinner-dance or a formal Annual General Meeting. He is the first to speak, and thus sets the tone for what is to follow. He can be jocular or dictatorial, longwinded or curt. The conduct of the meeting is really in his hands.

I can give you an example of bad chairmanship from my own experience. I had been engaged as Guest Speaker (the light entertainment), at a Christmas Dinner given to employees and staff of a small company, held at a good hotel. The dinner was festive, if predictable (you should have as many turkey dinners

as an after-dinner speaker eats in December!) and the right air of *bonhomie* pervaded throughout the meal.

When it came to the speeches however, the Chairman took his opportunity to harangue his company, and their escorts, for poor figures during the previous year, suggesting that not only was the future of any further Christmas celebration in the balance, but that many of those present would be out of a job swiftly if things didn't improve. You can imagine my feelings as I sat listening to the Chairman's tirade, knowing that I was supposed to follow it immediately with half an hour of fun and jollity! He now briskly announced me, when I had the formidable task of trying to amuse a now thoroughly humiliated and depressed audience whose mince pies and Christmas pudding were sitting like lead in their stomachs.

When I had finished and sat down, the proceedings were over, but few people stayed for a convivial drink afterwards and we all left quickly to celebrate what was left of the Christmas spirit in our own ways after the blighted dinner. Certainly the Chairman might have had a point to make, but he shouldn't have chosen a Christmas dinner at which to do it. Special meetings, Annual General Meetings or business conferences are the time for such pep talks, and the company in question wasted their money on the dinner as far as the guests were concerned.

Obviously, at a dinner-dance, the Chairman's job is simply to welcome people, make sure the formal toasts are proposed correctly, make a few observations himself in his short speech, and get the guest speakers on their feet efficiently.

At more formal meetings, the Chairman's responsibilities are greater. The Chairman at a meeting is there to see that the business gets done efficiently and fairly, and that it is seen to be so done. He has the power to change the order of the *agenda* (although he will be well advised to tell the meeting exactly why he has done so), and he can suggest that a topic has been debated long enough for the feeling of the meeting to have been tested. It must be obvious that at a meeting where serious issues are to be discussed, those attending must trust the Chairman to ensure that all shades of opinion are canvassed, and that no one speaker monopolizes the debate. It is to the Chair that all speakers address themselves initially, and in the event of the Chairman rising to his feet, the person currently speaking must give way.

Thus the Chairman has power, but how he exercises it is the important thing. He must have the *authority* about him to make clear to anyone tempted to break the rules of debate, that it won't be worth their while doing so. He must convince the meeting that even the most retiring and timid of speakers will be heard properly, and that those speakers experienced enough to exploit a situation are not over-indulged. He must do all this in a manner that will not turn the whole meeting against him.

Although the Chairman can in theory speak as often as he wishes, it would be inadvisable for him to do so. After his introductory remarks, he should try and leave it to those chosen to speak, relying on his authority to conduct the meeting with the voting on motions, and general progress.

The Chairman must also ensure that someone is taking proper *minutes* of the proceedings, and that that person gets the details and precise wording of all motions, with their Proposers and Seconders, properly set down. It helps the secretary if the Chairman recaps thoroughly at the end of each vote, that 'Such-and-such a motion was proposed by Jim Blades, and seconded by Mary Hobday, and carried unanimously', or whatever the case may be.

At most meetings common courtesy alone would suggest that all rules applying to the conduct of a meeting should be adhered to, but in the event of a speaker or a member of the audience ignoring such rules, it is up to the Chairman to *control* the situation.

THE DUTIES OF A CHAIRMAN

A businesslike but understanding approach should take the heat out of the most contentious debates, and humour is always a great disarmer, but if the situation really shows signs of getting out of control, the Chairman has the power to ask people to leave, or even to adjourn the meeting. A Chairman's skill may be measured by the manner in which a heated meeting is brought to order in everyone's best interests.

Thus we see that a Chairman can be a dictator, although it is much better that he should be a host, using courtesy and even humour to supplement his authority. Never should he display any sign of weakness. Vacillation and indecision on the Chairman's part will demoralize the whole meeting, and give the floor to anyone strong enough to have his own way.

Another problem that can arise for a Chairman is for him to gauge when any one subject has been debated enough. There are several ways open to him. He can back his own feelings and announce that due to pressure of time he will take three more speakers on this subject, and then put it to the vote. He can ask the meeting if they wish the matter to be debated any further, or he can move a closure. Often such a suggestion will come from the floor with a suggestion 'That the motion now be put'. Closures and calls for 'Progress' should be put to the vote if the meeting seems divided, and if the meeting decides that more time is needed to debate this subject, then so it must be, remembering that there is often a deadline by which the meeting must complete its agenda.

Companies and major business concerns have their own very strictly drawn-up rules of procedure for meetings, and the Chairman has to be guided by the Company Secretary if he has any doubts as to the way in which he should proceed.

It is in the smaller, less formal, meetings, that discretion is so important. As I write, I am Chairman of the Management Committee of a holiday hotel for handicapped children. There is not one person around that committee table who is not dedicated to the welfare of the children, and the prudent spending of the funds available. Each person is giving their services and time, and each is a busy person. I must therefore give everyone a hearing, and get a consensus feeling of the meeting. It would be pointless and self-defeating to antagonize or alienate any one member of the committee, and I am lucky in that our utlimate goal, the welfare of the children, prevents any deadlocks.

At the other end of the scale, political or Trade Union meetings tend to get so heated that mechanical devices have to be employed to ensure that fairness prevails. Television viewers will be familiar with the coloured lights over the speaker's lectern which indicate that green means 'Speak', amber means 'Two minutes left', and red means 'Get off', however emotional the speaker might appear to feel about the subject.

* * * *

To sum up, to be asked to be Chairman of any committee is an honour and a responsibility. While you are Chairman it is to you that letters will be addressed, to you that the Press will direct their attentions, and yours will be the hands that shake those of the famous if the occasion so dictates. Those are the rewards, coupled possibly with the knowledge that during your term of office you haven't done too much harm to the cause, and that your successor knows that he can do the job far better than you did.

Chapter Eight

IN THE OPEN AIR

It might well happen that you will be called upon to speak out of doors. I'm not thinking so much of political rallies, but more of garden fêtes, flower shows and gymkhanas that all need to be opened formally by a celebrity who has to be welcomed first and thanked afterwards.

The first rule is that even with the best of sound amplification equipment, and not many outdoor functions can boast that, a high wind can snatch your words clean away, so the keynote is *brevity*. Keep your speech very short indeed. Speak much more slowly than you usually would, and keep your sentences shorter. Open air speaking is very hard on the vocal cords, not just in the extra effort and volume needed in the voice, but with the effect of cool fresh air on the throat.

Nearly always at open air functions, your audience will be standing up, so it is essential that you have some sort of *raised platform* from which to speak in order that they might see you. The higher the better, and three or four feet at least. If no platform or makeshift stage is available, you can try the back of a truck or even risk your life by standing on a chair.

Al fresco speaking is definitely *not* the time for amusing anecdotes or subtle stories. They will simply evaporate in the air. Stand up, welcome those who have to be welcomed, thank those who have to be thanked, bang the drum for whatever good cause the function is in aid of, and sit down again.

Try not to be put off by your first sight of an outdoor audience. If you've become used to seeing orderly rows of attentive people sitting in a hall, or at tables at a dinner, the sudden spectacle of children and dogs weaving between people's legs, ladies in headscarves carrying on their conversation without even glancing at you, and men impatiently looking from their watches to the beer tent, might put you off.

Smile manfully, be brief, and be audible. I do realise that Dr Donald Soper could carry a large crowd in Hyde Park for hours on end, and that Michael Foot could get hundreds of people standing in a drizzle to cheer, but I would remind you that these are exceptionally practised orators, with a lifetime of experience on the hustings behind them. I suggest that the fact that you are reading this book at all indicates that you are not quite in their league, so please be guided.

Keeping any sort of dignity when on show in the open air is hard enough. Ladies in large floppy hats and billowing dresses trying to make their voices heard over the rain cascading down on the tent roofs have been a target for cartoonists for years. A famous comedian long ago warned me to try to avoid opening garden fêtes. He reckoned that however much you were reassured about the arrangements and the careful preparations beforehand, sooner or later you would wind up on the back of a haycart in a howling gale. The last time I saw him he had even had to pay to get in, as the person on the gate hadn't recognized him.

* * * *

Once again, try to imagine the worst thing that could happen to you under the circumstances, and be sure that it will.

Chapter Nine

RADIO AND TELEVISION
INTERVIEWS

In this age in which we have the constant daily barrage of four television channels (with even more promised), plus dozens of national and local radio stations, there is every chance that sooner or later you will either be asked to attend a studio to make a contribution to a programme, or else you will be accosted in the street by a person with a mike and a camera and asked to give your opinion on some matter of world-shattering importance. It is interesting to me that in these days of immediate mass communication we are all expected to be able to deliver an instant informed opinion on almost any topic, from the import of pig food to the question of life on Mars.

We are not all fluent and articulate when we have to think on our feet, and an incautious comment made under pressure but exposed possibly to millions, can be most damaging. My first instinct therefore is to ask for some time to consider your reply to the interviewer's question. In a studio, asked to talk on your own subject, you would probably be perfectly· in control. Nevertheless you would still be in a strange environment, amongst people well-skilled in getting the answers they want, or showing up any apparent weakness.

On the street, impromptu, my instinct would be to walk on and ignore the importuning interviewer—and I am not normally known for my reticence. However, the experience of sitting at home and watching some poor commuter interrupted on his way home in the middle of Oxford Street, his tie crooked and his hair unkempt,

stammering 'Oooh, er, well... it's wrong innit?', has cured me of wanting to express myself on the pavement.

Let's look at *radio interviews* more closely. A studio researcher has telephoned you and asked you to come in and talk on such-and-such a radio programme about a certain subject on which you might be able to give an expert opinion. You may be familiar with the programme and the way the interviews are carried out, but if you're not then you must somehow find out if the dialogue is likely to be sympathetic to you or hostile, and what stance the programme is likely to take. You must find out if what you are going to say is to go out live or to be recorded and possibly edited in a way that might cause some distortion.

Try to establish then, with the researcher on the 'phone, the context in which you are being asked to comment, i.e. is it a serious interview show, or are you to be some sort of filler between pop records? If you decide to go ahead, try to find out what the questions are likely to be. You can get your facts assembled and be prepared. You must also be ready for the loaded question, aimed to discredit what you say. This is not to suggest that all interviews are necessarily hostile, but frequently they can be. Your subject can also be treated with a flippancy you weren't expecting, and it's little good afterwards telling friends that 'you didn't really mean to say that'. Be prepared, and remember that you are doing them a favour by attending in the first place.

What sort of treatment can you expect to receive when you get to the studio? It will vary, of course, with the size and prestige of the radio station, but usually you will be met at reception by a researcher, probably the one you first spoke to on the 'phone. You will be conducted to the studio area which usually has two rooms, one in which the actual interview will take place, equipped with a table, chairs, a few mikes, headphones, possibly record-playing apparatus, and generally a feeling of too much stuff in too confined a space. The other room will be the production room in

71

which sit the producer and the technicians responsible for seeing the show on the air. You will normally be taken to this room first where the producer will brief you, maybe give you a cup of coffee, and keep you until the moment when the presenter is ready for you.

When you do finally get into the actual studio there will not normally be much time for a talk with the presenter before you start the actual interview. The producer from the production room will probably ask you to say a few words into the mike to give the sound engineer a level for volume—and then you'll be off. You understand, then, why I urge you to be fully equipped in your own mind as to what you are going to say, and to have all the facts immediately to hand, in note form if necessary.

If you are to be in a *television studio*, much the same applies, except that there is far more equipment around, and there will be many more people. There will be the men operating cameras, the sound men, and a floor manager whose job it will be to make sure that you are sitting in the right chair at the right time. A make-up girl will probably come in and powder your face a bit, and you might get the chance to comb your hair and straighten your clothes. I'm discussing now the 'newsy' sort of show. The bigger interview shows will give you much more time for repose.

In all cases, as I've said, you will be in a new and bewildering world, and one in which just about everyone except you knows exactly what is going to happen. Nevertheless, it is you that they wish to talk to, and so you are entitled to take a deep breath or two, and consider each question carefully before you answer it. I'm going to repeat one other bit of earlier advice, and urge against the temptation to have a swift drink or two on the way to the studio—or even at the studio if the hospitality goes that far. Over-confidence may lead you to indiscretion, and on colour television even a couple of scotches give quite a glow to the cheeks.

Interviews on radio or TV can be fun, and certainly let

you reach a wider audience for your views than you would normally be able to expect. One more point though. Despite the possible millions listening or viewing, remember that you are talking only to one—the interviewer. It is a dialogue on which others are eavesdropping.

A comparatively new phenomenon has entered the world of interviews, that of the *phone-in*. On such radio shows you talk not only with the interviewer, but by the use of headphones can answer questions directly to people telephoning into the programme. I have a pad of paper and a thick pen beside me on such shows on which I immediately write the name of the caller so that I can call him by name during the chat.

In many studios there is a device which allows a time lag of a few seconds between the conversation in the studio and its actual transmission to the public. This gives the producer the chance to discard the possible use of obscenities or causes for writs of libel action. It is for the broadcasting company's own protection, and need not concern you at all, other than to know the protection exists.

Should you be asked to go to a studio to record a *piece of your own*, maybe a quarter of an hour on your own subject, refer back to my comments on the rehearsing of a speech with a tape recorder. This way, not only do you know you will be within your allowed time, but you will have been able to discard any verbal traps such as difficult words over which you might stumble, or a clumsy-sounding sentence. On this sort of radio talk I advocate having the entire piece in written form, typed double-spaced on a good typewriter. With such a script, should you have to go back over a bit for technical reasons, you can pick it up immediately, without having to collect your thoughts.

In short then, radio and television can be wonderful slaves, but terrible masters. It is entirely up to you whether you want to use such media in the first place—you can still say the magic word 'No'. However, if you do decide to expose yourself to the millions, then do your best to see that you are in control of the situation.

Chapter Ten
TURNING PROFESSIONAL

Up until now I have assumed that your speech was to be a piece prepared for one special occasion only, but let us consider the situation that might arise should you suddenly find that your speech is such a big success that other organizations want you to deliver it for them, to such an extent that quite a chunk of your time will be allocated simply to being a public speaker. Under such circumstances it is only right that you should be rewarded for your efforts, above the usual dinner and expenses money.

Putting yourself on to a professional basis as a speaker is a gradual process, work being generated usually by that best of publicity media, word-of-mouth. Someone present when you speak thinks that you would be suitable for his own function and approaches you, and after doing his function a couple more people ask you to theirs; so you build up a connection.

Setting the Fee

At this point you must try to decide the level of fee that seems appropriate to you. It is not now simply a matter of a social night out, possibly with a partner, but of travelling long distances and perhaps staying the night. All of this will take you away from your normal working pattern, and you must consider all the hours you are going to be away when assessing a fee, not just the half hour you spend actually speaking. How much is your time worth to you at an hourly rate, adding on travelling time?

It's not easy to come to a figure which adequately compensates you for your time and expertise, and yet which can be afforded by organizations for your services. You may either opt for setting yourself a standard fee and never varying it, or you might feel like cutting your coat according to the cloth available, asking a small fee for a small club in a village hall and a bigger sum for a posh do at the Hilton. This really has to be your own decision, and the only real advice you can get is from the organizers of functions who know what they've paid out to previous speakers, and what the 'market level' is.

Getting Publicity

As I've said, the word-of-mouth publicity of being personally recommended from dinner to dinner is the best of all, and the only one of value in the long run. However, if requests for your services really do start coming in heavily, you might think it worthwhile to have some small brochures printed, with details of your talk, maybe a favourable press clipping or two if available, and a picture of yourself taken *recently*. That last item is important; a snapshot of you taken thirty years ago in Cromer really will not be suitable. It has been known for a speaker expecting to be met at the station to be left on the platform because those picking him up failed to recognize him from his picture. Brochures cost quite a bit of money, and unless you are looking seriously at making public speaking a part of your livelihood, it is as well to think hard before spending the money.

Finding an Agent

There are a very few specialized agencies around the country who place speakers into suitable functions, but invariably they will make the approach to you. The rueful old showbusiness saying of 'Don't call us—we'll call you', applies in this case too. If you have something to offer on a professional basis, sooner or later one of the agencies will contact you. By the very nature of their business they keep closely in touch with their

76

various contacts, and any new bright speaker will be brought to their attention quickly. Your local Yellow Pages directory might list such an agent, and you might think it worth while sending them details of your offering, but please believe me that they will call you very swiftly if they need you.

Most agents charge a commission on the fee they negotiate for you. Usually it is between ten and fifteen percent. Your expenses money is not subject to such commission. Once in a while you might be offered a fee by an agent that is not subject to commission—he might talk of a 'net' figure. This can be a sign that the agent is going to add a hefty chunk of his own to your fee from the booker. Don't be surprised—you can turn down the job if you don't like the terms.

The acceptance of a fee will put heavier obligations on you than you might have realized. Often organizations will book up to a year ahead and your name will appear on their printed list of forthcoming events. By your contract with them you are bound to appear, and only extreme sickness can be expected to be taken as a reason for your not turning up on the night in question. If you fail to turn up more than once, the word will go out that you are unreliable, and if you have been booked by an agency they will drop you, however good your speech.

Remember too that any fees you may earn as a speaker will be subject to Income Tax, and will have to be declared. Great are the penalties for not doing so. More than one speaker has felt secure in travelling miles from his home to a small function in the country and feeling sufficiently anonymous to consider slipping his fee into his pocket and not declaring it, only to learn later that numbered amongst his audience that night was a local and inquisitive taxman.

* * * *

The rewards of travelling around the country with a good suit and a good speech can be great, and not only in financial terms. It is worth thinking very hard, however, before undertaking such a venture as a part of your everyday income. Certainly you mustn't throw up a steady employment in exchange for what might well be only a shortlived flash of fame. Mortgages last a long time....

QUOTATIONS

Dick Turpin, in another context, coined the best quotation for any public speaker when he declaimed 'Stand and Deliver'. Most people have their own favourite quotations or proverbs which they tend to use throughout their lives. Sometimes these span whole generations, as my old Grandad used to say. However, to set you thinking a bit, and even to save you a little time in research, I've set down a few suitable quotations which you might be able to use, and to make it even easier for you, I've set them under headings that might be encountered by speakers.

Advertising

Advertising may be described as the science of arresting the human intelligence long enough to get money from it.

Stephen Leacock

Advertising is the rattling of a stick inside a swill bucket.

George Orwell

Advertising is the art of making whole lies out of half truths.

Edgar A. Shoaff

Advertisements contain the only truths to be relied on in a newspaper.

Thomas Jefferson

Business

Do other men for they would do you. That's the true business precept.

Charles Dickens

QUOTATIONS

The business of America is business.

Calvin Coolidge

If the government was as afraid of disturbing the consumer as it is of disturbing business, this would be some democracy.

'Kin Hubbard'

There are two times in a man's life when he should not speculate: when he can't afford it and when he can.

Mark Twain

Statistics indicate that, as a result of overwork, modern executives are dropping like flies on the nation's golf courses.

Ira Wallach

I think that there is nothing, not even crime, more opposed to poetry, to philosophy, ay, to life itself than this incessant business.

Thoreau

Ethics

An ethical man is a Christian holding four aces.

Mark Twain

I would rather be the man who bought the Brooklyn Bridge than the man who sold it.

Will Rogers

What is moral is what you feel good after.

E. Hemingway

An Englishman thinks he is moral when he is only uncomfortable.

G. B. Shaw

Fame

The day will come when everyone will be famous for fifteen minutes.

Andy Warhol

Fame is the spur.

Milton

Man dreams of fame while woman wakes to love.

Tennyson

A celebrity is a person who works hard all his life to become well known, and then wears dark glasses to avoid being recognised.

Fred Allen

If fame is to come only after death, I am in no hurry for it.

Marcus Valerius Martial (AD 40-102)

Family

If you cannot get rid of the family skeleton, you may as well make it dance.

G. B. Shaw

Most parents don't worry about a daughter until she fails to show up for breakfast. Then it is too late.

'Kin Hubbard'

To bring up a child in the way he should go, travel that way yourself once in a while.

Josh Billings

Some people seem compelled by unkind fate to parental servitude for life. There is no form of penal servitude much worse than this.

Samuel Butler

Golf

If you watch a game, it's fun. If you play it, it's recreation. If you work at it, it's golf.

Bob Hope

Golf is a good walk spoiled.

Mark Twain

The only reason I ever played golf in the first place was so I could afford to hunt and fish.

Sam Snead

Marriage

Marriage is a great institution, but I'm not ready for an institution yet.

Mae West

The critical period in matrimony is breakfast time.

A.P. Herbert

A man in love is incomplete until he has married. Then he's finished.

Zsa Zsa Gabor

Niagara Falls is only the second biggest disappointment of the standard honeymoon.

Oscar Wilde

Money

As a general rule, nobody has money who ought to have it.

B. Disraeli

It is not the employer who pays wages—he only handles the money. It's the product that pays wages.

Henry Ford

When a fellow says, 'It ain't the money but the principle of the thing', it's the money.

'Kin Hubbard'

Never invest your money in anything that eats or needs repairing.

Billy Rose

Old Age

When a man retires and time is no longer a matter of urgent importance, his colleagues generally present him with a watch.

R.C. Sheriff

You know you are getting old when the candles cost more than the cake.

Bob Hope

Forty is the old age of youth; fifty the youth of old age.

Victor Hugo

When your friends begin to flatter you on how young you look, it's a sure sign you're getting old.

Mark Twain

On the Use of Quotations

The wisdom of the wise and the experience of the ages are perpetuated by quotations.

B. Disraeli

I often quote myself. It adds spice to my conversation.

G.B. Shaw

I quote others only the better to express myself.

M. de Montaigne

It is a good thing for an uneducated man to read books of quotations.

Winston Churchill

QUOTATIONS

Travel

A good holiday is one spent among people whose notions of time are vaguer than yours.

J.B. Priestly

In America there are two classes of travel—first class and with children.

Robert Benchley

See one promontory, one mountain, one sea, one river, and see all.

Plato (427-347 BC)

A tourist is a fellow who drives thousands of miles so he can be photographed standing in front of his car.

Emile Ganest

Airline travel is hours of boredom interrupted by moments of stark terror.

Al Boliska

* * * *

These, then, are a few quotations you might feel like using some time in your public pronouncements. You might have noticed that I've avoided the very obvious sources, such as The Bible and Shakespeare, in an attempt to bring some newer names in. Perhaps my final wish should be that your own public speeches will become so successful that in a few years' time, I shall be quoting you.

USEFUL BOOKS

Suggested further reading, either for reference or research

Burchfield, Robert, *The Spoken Word,* BBC Publications, 1981

Castle, Dennis, and Wade, John, *Public Speaking,* Teach Yourself Books, Hodder and Stoughton, 1980

Encyclopaedia of Dates and Events, Teach Yourself Books, Hodder and Stoughton, 1974

Goodworth, C.T., *Effective Speaking and Presentation for the Company Executive,* Business Books, 1980

Gowers, Sir Ernest, *Plain Words,* H.M.S.O.

Oxford Dictionary of Quotations, Oxford University Press, 1974

Roget's Thesaurus, Penguin, 1970

Who's Who, A and C Black, published annually

INDEX

INDEX